A DAY THAT CHANGED AMERICA

THE ALAMO

MARCH 6, 1836

A DAY THAT CHANGED AMERICA
THE ALAMO

Surrounded and Outnumbered,
They Chose to Make a Defiant Last Stand

TEXT BY SHELLEY TANAKA ❧ PAINTINGS BY DAVID CRAIG

Historical consultation by Dr. Bruce Winders

A SCHOLASTIC / MADISON PRESS BOOK

It didn't look like much of a fortress. Its walls were low and broken, a patchwork of stone, mud, and timbers. A narrow ditch ran around the outside. Beyond the ditch lay gently rolling fields dotted with orchards and clumps of mesquite. On the other side of a winding river was San Antonio de Béjar, a sleepy little town of flat-roofed adobe houses, dusty plazas, and domed churches.

But the crumbling fort was a rebel stronghold, and on March 6, 1836, it would become a fierce and bloody battleground.

WAGONS WEST

BY THE BEGINNING OF THE 1500S, EUROPEANS HAD STARTED TO ARRIVE IN THE AMERICAS. Spain, Portugal, France, and England all wanted to expand their empires. They sent settlers to the New World to seek out rich farmland, gold, silver, timber, and furs.

The settlers built towns and cities and raised families for many generations. Eventually, the colonists did not want to be ruled by the faraway countries that controlled them. In the 1770s, in the east, the thirteen colonies battled England in the War for American Independence. Later, in the south, Mexico won its independence from Spain in a war that gave Mexico control over Texas — a vast, unsettled territory.

The newly formed United States began to look beyond the original thirteen colonies for trade and land. People like Thomas Jefferson even imagined a single great country that would one day extend all the way to the Pacific Ocean. It would be a nation where everyone spoke the same language and was governed in the same way.

In the early 1800s, Americans began to move west. Thousands of them poured over the Mexican border into Texas. The land was dirt cheap — as little as twelve and a half cents an acre in some places.

Mexico welcomed the newcomers at first, but soon realized these settlers were a threat. The Americans did not speak Spanish. They kept slaves, which was against Mexican law. They did not want to pay taxes. And they brought their friends and families, until there were almost ten American-born "Texians" for every Mexican-born Tejano.

The Mexican government wanted to stop the flow of Americans moving into Texas. The Texians wanted to be free from Mexican rule, so they called for volunteers from the

New Land, New Beginnings

Spain once claimed more than half of present-day United States. After Mexico gained independence from Spain in 1821, it still controlled a large part of North America that extended west to the Pacific Ocean and north to the Oregon Country. But the U.S. was determined to expand into Mexican territory. Thousands of settlers moved from the U.S. into the Mexican colony of Texas, and by 1836 these American-born Texians wanted independence from Mexican rule. After many years of fighting, Texas (shown in red) became a new state in 1845. The U.S. gained control of the disputed area to the west of it in 1848.

United States to bring their rifles and help them fight for Texian independence. They wanted Texas to be an independent state.

In December 1835, a rebel army of Texians drove Mexican troops out of San Antonio de Béjar and took over the Alamo, one of the most important posts in northern Mexico. It was a tense and angry situation that was bound to explode.

And explode it did. On February 23, 1836, about fifteen hundred Mexican soldiers, led by their fearsome president, General Antonio López de Santa Anna Perez de Lebron,

From Hero to Tyrant

In March of 1836, Antonio López de Santa Anna Perez de Lebron was forty-two years old and had been president of Mexico for three years. He had fought against Spain's attempt to reconquer Mexico in 1829 and been hailed as a hero. This helped him become president four years later. But soon after he was elected, Santa Anna decided that Mexico was not ready to be governed by its own people.

He also feared the Texians' growing demands and suspected the colonists would eventually want Texas to join the United States. It was not long before the American and Tejano colonists began to rebel against his government.

When a band of Texians seized the Alamo, Santa Anna was furious. He led his troops on a long march across hundreds of miles from San Luis Potosi to San Antonio.

rode into San Antonio to take the Alamo back into Mexican hands. About two hundred Texian rebels, along with some women and children, shut themselves up in the Alamo. They immediately fired on the Mexican troops.

The rebels refused to surrender. Santa Anna vowed that the Texians would never leave the fort alive.

Both sides held their ground for twelve long days, but it was a standoff that could not continue. On March 5, Santa Anna decided it was time to take back the Alamo — at any cost.

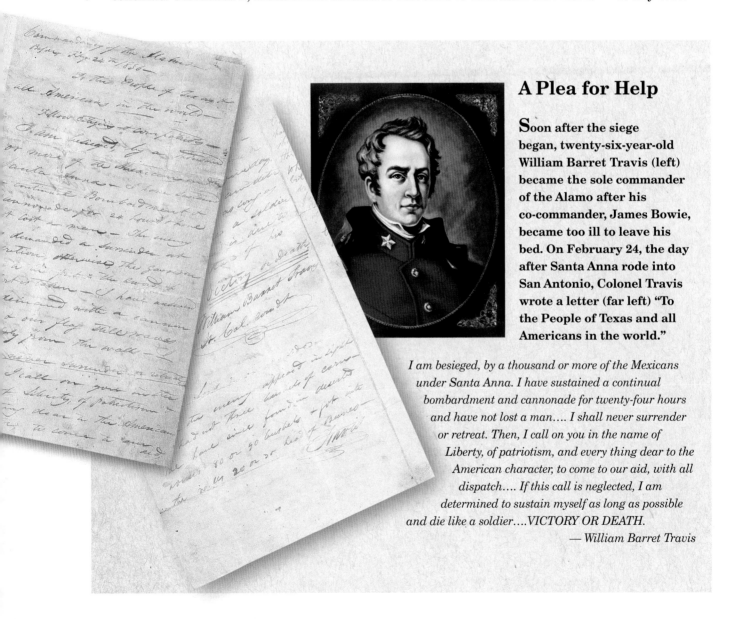

A Plea for Help

Soon after the siege began, twenty-six-year-old William Barret Travis (left) became the sole commander of the Alamo after his co-commander, James Bowie, became too ill to leave his bed. On February 24, the day after Santa Anna rode into San Antonio, Colonel Travis wrote a letter (far left) "To the People of Texas and all Americans in the world."

I am besieged, by a thousand or more of the Mexicans under Santa Anna. I have sustained a continual bombardment and cannonade for twenty-four hours and have not lost a man…. I shall never surrender or retreat. Then, I call on you in the name of Liberty, of patriotism, and every thing dear to the American character, to come to our aid, with all dispatch…. If this call is neglected, I am determined to sustain myself as long as possible and die like a soldier….VICTORY OR DEATH.
— *William Barret Travis*

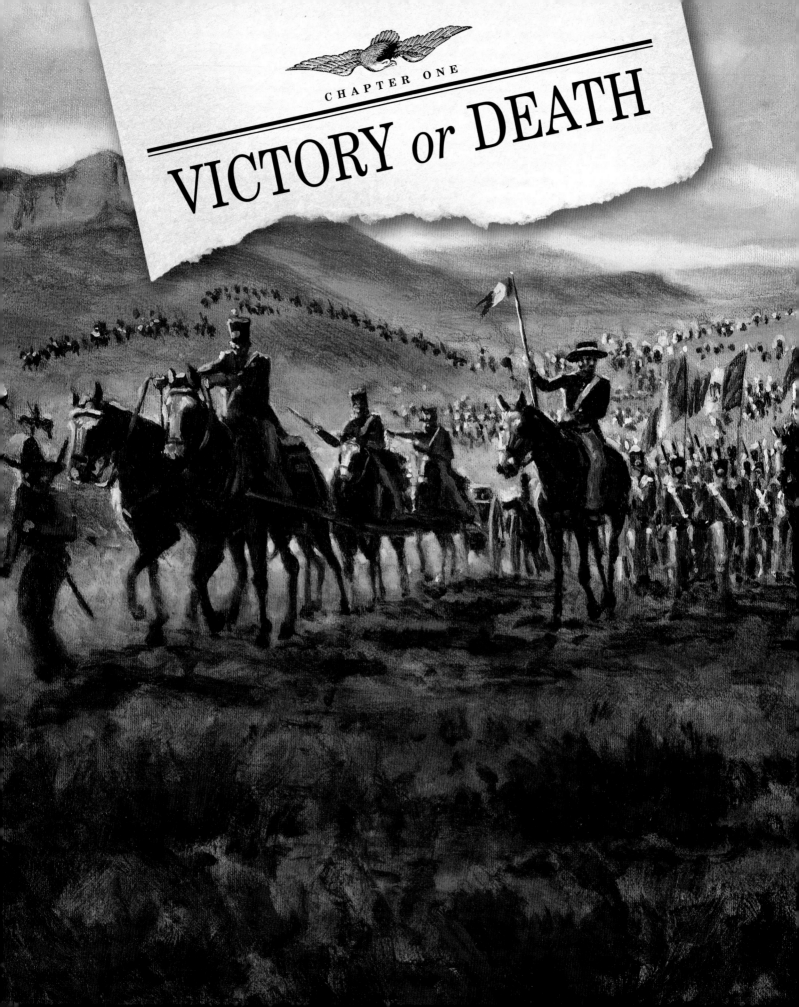

CHAPTER ONE

VICTORY or DEATH

By the time Santa Anna's troops reached the Alamo, they were exhausted and hungry. They had traveled hundreds of miles in bitter winter weather — braving rugged terrain, with hardly any food or water.

It was just past midnight on March 6, 1836, when President Santa Anna and his chief of staff, Colonel Juan Almonte, rode out to check their troops. Their horses made a wide circle around the Alamo, well out of earshot of the Texian rebels holed up in the fort.

It was time for Santa Anna's officers to wake the troops. The men had been sleeping since dusk. They would need that rest. In just a few hours, they would attack the fort.

The men stirred and made themselves ready. They counted their cartridges and flints, and fixed bayonets to their muskets. They cast off their blankets, though the night air was cold. The president's orders were very clear. No capes or overcoats. Chin straps had to be fastened tight. Shoes had to be worn. Ladder carriers were to have their rifles slung over their shoulders. Smoking was forbidden.

It was crucial that the Texians did not hear, see, or smell them. Everyone was to move in absolute silence. Not a single shot was to be fired until the trenches of the Alamo had been reached and the Mexican soldiers were right under the nose of the enemy. When the bugle sounded to launch the attack, nothing must stop them from moving as quickly as possible.

The Mexican *soldados* gathered in their formations and moved to the narrow wooden bridges that crossed the river. The houses of San Antonio were dark and empty. Many of the townspeople had already loaded up their oxcarts with their belongings, buried their money, and hustled their families out of town. Everyone knew the battle, when it came, would be bloody and merciless.

And the time for battle had come. Santa Anna would take the Alamo back from the Texian rebels and their American friends who had come with their guns to chase Mexicans off their land. They were nothing but pirates and lawless foreigners who had fired on Mexican troops on Mexican soil.

By 2:00 a.m., the Mexican troops had the Alamo surrounded. Cavalry units waited to the east, in case any Texians tried to escape. Other companies guarded supplies and secured the lines of communication back to Mexico City.

The battle had not yet begun, but Santa Anna had already lost many men. For two months, he had marched his army across several rivers and the cold, dry plains of south Texas. Many had not survived the journey. Now the men inside the Alamo had held out for much longer than he had expected. Many Mexicans had been shot down by the Texians during the siege.

He had to admit that Colonel Travis and his men were brave. They fought like tigers, especially the tall man they called Crockett. He was constantly firing from the wooden palisade at the front of the church. He rarely missed, and Santa Anna's men always kept a good distance whenever they saw him. He would shout curses at them, and even though the Mexican *soldados* could not understand him, they knew he was taunting them.

(Above) Santa Anna's army was made up of cavalrymen on horseback as well as infantrymen or foot soldiers. A professional soldier (right) wore a uniform modeled after that of the French army — although the circular design on top of the hat and winged epaulets on the shoulders were unique to the Mexican uniform.

Santa Anna and Colonel Almonte finished checking the troops and circled back to their headquarters in town. Almonte was worried. He knew the generals were uncertain about the coming battle. The officers wanted to wait for the Texians to surrender rather than send so many of their men to certain death. The fort could not hold out much longer. The Texians only had a limited supply of food, ammunition, and water.

But Santa Anna was firm. The time for surrender was past. His spies told him that Texian reinforcements could arrive at any moment. He would not wait any longer.

Almonte turned to Santa Anna. "This will cost us much," he said.

The president looked at him with eyes that were bright with anger. "It must be done," he replied. "The Alamo must fall, and my orders will be obeyed. If our soldiers are driven back, the next line must push those before them, and force them to scale the walls, no matter what the cost."

INSIDE THE ALAMO, ALL WAS QUIET. THE TEXIAN DEFENDERS HAD FALLEN INTO AN EXHAUSTED sleep. Even the soldiers on watch were dozing at their posts. There was nothing much to see. The fires of the Mexican camps glowed in the distance. No doubt the *soldados* were sleeping, too.

In the corner of the sacristy of the Alamo's church, eight-year-old Enrique Esparza tossed on his straw mat. He had lived in San Antonio his whole life, and Texas was his home. Could he not be loyal to Mexico and Texas at the same time? His uncle was a soldier in Santa Anna's army. Did that mean he was the enemy?

If the Texians defeated Santa Anna, Enrique could go home. His friends would come back to town, and life would be the way it was before. Most Tejano families had left weeks earlier, when they had first heard that Santa Anna was coming. Others left the fort after the siege began. The Tejano people did not want to leave their homes, but they were afraid of fighting alongside so many Americans, because Santa Anna despised Americans.

Enrique's father, Gregorio, was friends with James Bowie, one of the Alamo commanders. He wanted to stay and fight with him. Gregorio told Enrique's mother, Ana, to take the family away to a safer place, but she refused. Instead, she took charge of the other women and children in the fort. She ground corn and boiled it in water for their meals. When they were too frightened to eat, she practically poured it down their throats to make sure they kept up their strength.

A Man of Honor

James Bowie was famous as the greatest knife fighter in the country long before he fought at the Alamo. The huge curved hunting knife that he always carried was crafted by his brother, Rezin Bowie, and became known as the Bowie knife. As tales of James Bowie's fearless dueling spread, men all over the southern states had Bowie knives (like the one at left) made for themselves.

In 1830, Bowie went to live in Texas, where he soon became a Mexican citizen, converted to the Catholic faith, and settled in San Antonio. He married a Mexican woman named Ursula de Veramendi, the daughter of the vice governor of Coahuila and Texas, and became well known among the Tejano people in Texas.

When the Alamo was seized by the Texian rebels, the post commander wrote to American commander-in-chief Sam Houston to ask for help. Houston sent Bowie to the Alamo to check on the situation. Bowie agreed that the fortress had to be defended, and he also thought it would be useful in the fight for Texas. He joined the rebels and, in a letter to Sam Houston, wrote, "We will rather die in these ditches than give it up to the enemy."

Enrique remembered the afternoon Santa Anna had ridden into town, thirteen long days before. The boy had never seen such a splendid sight. The horsemen wore scarlet coats and leather helmets. Their swords and lances glinted in the late afternoon sun and the plumes on their helmets waved in the breeze. The battalions at the front marched in neat rows. Behind them came mules and teams of men hauling heavy black cannons. Flags fluttered in the cool breeze, and the musicians played.

*Santa Anna, right, and soldiers
of the Mexican army.*

At the front was the Mexican president himself, sitting tall in his saddle. He looked magnificent, his gold epaulets gleaming. Then the president got down from his horse, and Enrique saw his face. His dark hair was swept forward over his broad forehead. His piercing eyes were as black as steel.

Enrique had turned and run home, where his parents were hastily gathering together cooking utensils and bags of food. The Esparza family had scarcely made it over the river and into the Alamo before Santa Anna's bugle sounded and a blood-red flag was raised on the top of the town church.

There was no mistaking the flag's message. Santa Anna would take no prisoners. If he won the coming battle, every man in the Alamo would die.

Now Enrique looked at the sleeping bodies lying around him. His sister and brothers were sound asleep. Several families were crowded into the small, airless room. Even through the thick stone walls of the church, he could smell the overflowing latrines and filthy cattle pens outside.

Were they all going to die? How could two hundred men fight off the mighty Mexican army?

He glanced with envy at twelve-year-old Benjamin Wolfe sleeping beside him, a rifle at his side. Enrique wished he had a weapon, but he was small for his age, and people still treated him like a baby. If he had a rifle, he could fight, too, just like his father and the new man who had arrived in town only a month earlier — David Crockett.

Enrique loved Señor Crockett. He was brave and funny and he didn't dress like the other men. He wore a buckskin jacket and a coonskin cap with a long tail hanging down the back. Enrique could not understand everything he said, but he loved the way Crockett joked and told stories, just like a Tejano. Señor Travis always looked sad and stern, but not Crockett. In the darkest days of the siege, when they were all wondering whether help would ever come, he would pull out his fiddle and play a rollicking tune, until they were all clapping and laughing.

Enrique was sure that nothing truly bad could happen with a man like David Crockett around to help them.

King of the Wild Frontier

By the time David Crockett came to Texas at the age of forty-nine, he was already famous as a soldier, hunter, congressman, and writer.

Born in a log cabin in eastern Tennessee in 1786, "Davy" Crockett grew up hunting in the woods around his home and quickly learned how to survive in the wild. He joined the military when he was twenty-five, and soon stories of his bravery and skill with a rifle spread throughout the states. Years later, he became a congressman, and continued to impress everyone with tales of bear hunting and backwoods adventures.

But in 1835, Crockett lost his bid for re-election to Congress. Disappointed and fed up with politics, he traveled to Texas in search of land and business opportunities. He arrived in San Antonio just weeks before the siege of the Alamo. Eager to help in the fight for Texas independence, he decided to join the defenders inside the fortress.

This portrait of David Crockett (above) was painted in 1886. It shows him dressed in his legendary buckskin clothing and holding a coonskin cap and rifle. Crockett also wore this colorful beaded vest (right) before he came to Texas. (Left) This rifle belonged to Crockett and is similar to the one he used at the Alamo.

Sometimes Enrique would sneak outside the sacristy, though his mother didn't like it. It was dangerous out in the open courtyard. At any moment, a shell from one of the Mexican howitzers could come soaring over the wall. Dust and stones and sharp pieces of metal would fly up and start fires in the grass.

Sometimes Enrique went with his mother to visit their friend Señor Bowie. He spoke Spanish, and Enrique felt safe with him.

But Bowie was sick. These days, his coughing could be heard all the way out in the courtyard. And even though he kept telling Señor Travis, "Help will come," it did not come.

ACROSS THE ROOM IN THE SACRISTY, SUSANNA DICKINSON SAT ON HER BED NURSING HER BABY girl, Angelina. Susanna, too, was remembering the day her husband, Almaron, had galloped up to their house with the news that Santa Anna's army was in town.

"Give me the baby!" Almaron had shouted. "Jump up behind me and ask no questions!" As they rode out of town and across the San Antonio River, she heard the Mexican army firing behind them.

She had come away with nothing. She had even torn up her apron to make diapers for the baby.

Now she and Angelina were living in the sacristy of the Alamo with the families of Gregorio Esparza and Anthony Wolfe, two of Almaron's fellow artillerymen. While the men manned the cannons at the top of the dirt ramp that had been built inside the church, the women and children took shelter below in the dark room.

Susanna worried about her husband up at his post. He was scarcely protected by the tattered walls of the fortress. But it was almost worse being inside, listening to the cannons roar above her, feeling the ground tremble. She knew the Mexicans were building ladders in full view of the fort. They were moving their encampments closer each day and tightening their noose around the Alamo.

Susanna spent her days looking after Angelina and cooking. The women made countless tortillas and roasted freshly killed beef over open fires for the men in the garrison. Other times she helped to nurse James Bowie. He had been in Texas far longer than most of the Americans — almost six years. He was too weak to leave his bed, yet his pistols never left his hands.

Susanna knew there was little hope left. Even David Crockett was worried about being pressed on all sides by enemy forces.

"I think we had better march out and die in the open air," he said. "I don't like to be hemmed up."

And now Colonel Travis seemed to be giving up. Earlier that evening, he had come to the church and sat little Angelina on his knee. Susanna's skin had prickled with fear when he placed a cat's-eye ring on a string around the baby's neck. The ring was made of hammered gold, and Susanna knew it had been a gift from the sweetheart Travis had left behind. Did Travis really believe that he would not live to see her again?

Colonel Travis holds up the shiny ring for Angelina to see.

As Santa Anna was preparing his troops outside, Colonel Travis was still awake in his headquarters at the west wall of the Alamo. On the other side of the room, his slave, Joe, was already asleep.

The entire garrison was exhausted, worn down by two weeks of defending the fort. Holding off the Mexicans was only half the battle. There were horses to care for and cattle to butcher. Artillery and ammunition had to be moved and counted. They had to dig new wells inside the fort as the Mexican forces drew closer. It had become too dangerous to make runs outside the walls for water and firewood. As the Mexican cannons tore more holes in the crumbling fort, the men worked late into the night digging trenches and piling earth and timbers against the outer walls. Long after dark, the Mexican troops fired their muskets into the air, shouting and jeering at the exhausted defenders, and blowing their bugles to keep them sleepless.

At least today had been quiet. There had scarcely been any firing all afternoon.

Still, Travis knew he could not hold out much longer. So this evening he had gathered the men together and given them a choice. They could stand with him and fight to the death, or they could leave. Only one man had decided not to stay, and he was long gone over the walls now.

Travis was bitter at the number of Tejanos who had fled the fort in the early days of the siege. Now only a handful of them remained. He had fewer than two hundred men altogether. Most were American citizens like himself and recent arrivals like Crockett. These were men who understood what they were fighting for — the right to be free of that dictator Santa Anna, the right to make new lives for themselves in their chosen land, and the right to have a say in how they would be governed.

Travis was prepared to die if he had to, but he was dismayed that his pleas for help had not yet been answered. Why hadn't America and the rest of Texas come to their assistance? Didn't they understand that if Santa Anna took the Alamo, he would push on, all the way to the American border?

Travis leaned his shotgun against the head of his bed and pulled the blanket up over his clothes. At dawn, he would fire the eighteen-pounder, the biggest cannon in the fort. It was his signal to let the world know that he was still holding the Alamo. He would not lose hope.

As his men and the remaining civilians in the fort gather solemnly around him, Colonel Travis explains that the fight is now to the death.

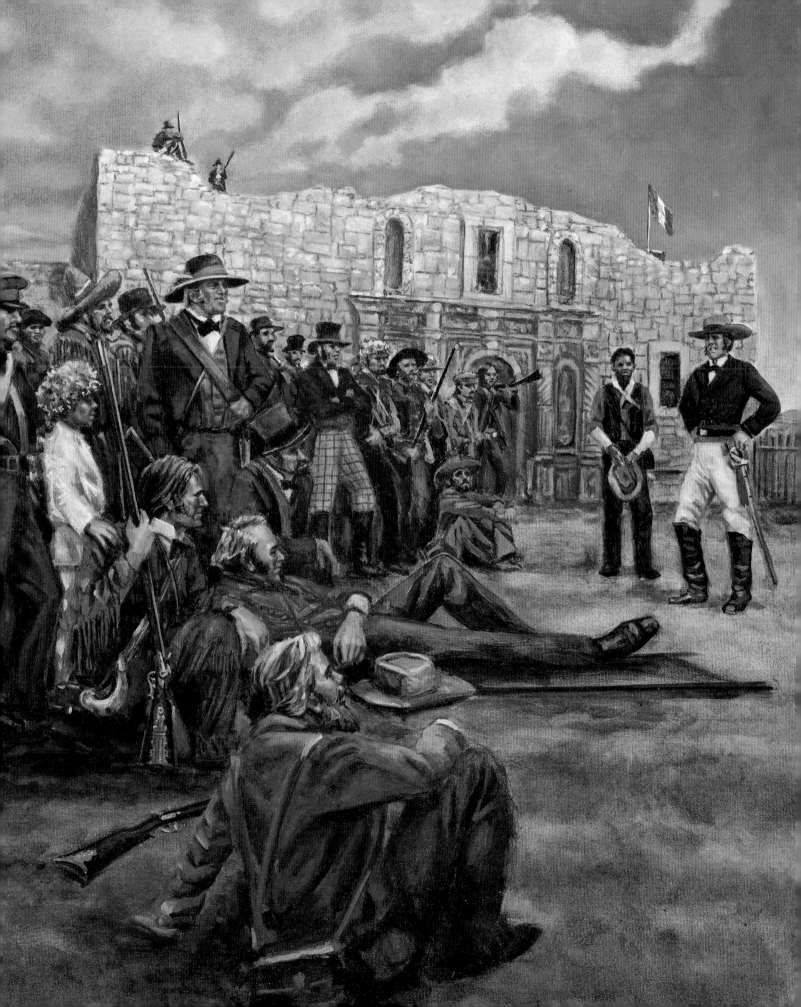

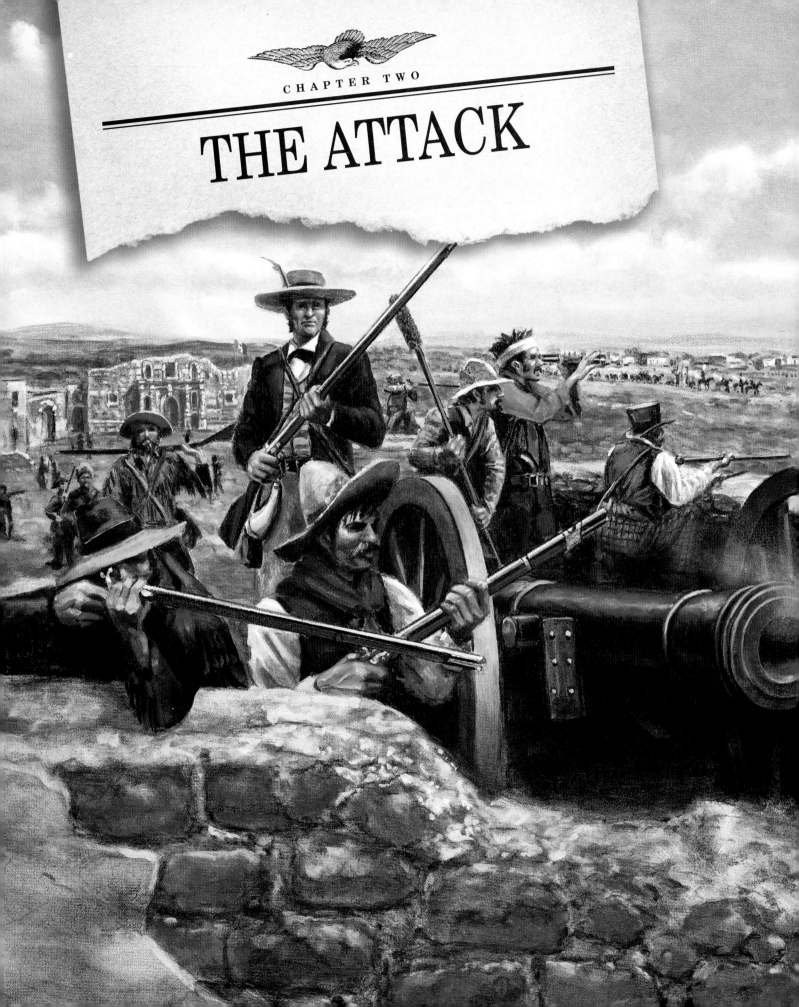

CHAPTER TWO

THE ATTACK

SANTA ANNA'S TROOPS WERE READY TO ATTACK LONG BEFORE DAWN. FOUR COLUMNS OF soldiers had the fort surrounded — two to the north and northwest, one to the east, and one to the south. Slightly farther back to the northeast stood the northern battery, where Santa Anna himself waited with his reserve troops. Sheltered behind an earthen barrier and flanked by cannons and howitzers, he was well protected. He also had a good view of the north wall.

Scarcely nine feet high, the north wall had been reinforced on the outside with sturdy wooden timbers and planks. Even without ladders, Santa Anna's men could easily climb into the fort — if they could reach the wall before the Texians spotted them.

He gave the signal to advance. The men crouched low. Some carried ladders, crowbars, spikes, and axes.

The troops began to move slowly forward under the cover of darkness. It was very quiet. Not even the crows had started their predawn cries. The men breathed quickly. Finally, the waiting was over.

But the tension was too much. Against orders, some of the men quickened their pace, and suddenly they were crashing over the mesquite-studded fields.

"Viva México!" a voice shouted, and then others joined in. *"Viva Santa Anna!"* Their battle cries drifted over the walls of the sleeping fort.

The enemy was alerted now. Santa Anna was furious, but he had to act quickly. There was no longer any reason for secrecy. He gave the signal to the regimental musicians behind him. The bugles sounded, and across the river a rocket shot into the black sky to mark the beginning of the attack.

Inside the Alamo, only the officer of the day was awake, but he wasted no time.

"The Mexicans are coming!" he shouted. Colonel Travis was out of bed in an instant. He called to Joe, seized his shotgun and sword, and rushed out into the courtyard. Joe grabbed his gun and followed Colonel Travis out of the room.

The two men ran to the north wall and climbed the steps to the rampart where the cannons waited. Already the rest of the defenders were swarming to the walls, clutching their arms, and taking their positions.

A day before the final attack, one of the defenders scans the horizon with a spyglass — looking for any sign that help is on the way.

"Come on, boys," Travis called out. "The Mexicans are upon us, and we'll give them hell!"

Enrique's father, Gregorio, and Almaron Dickinson ran to their crowded post at the top of the ramp in the church. They took turns firing their cannons against the column coming out from the trees to the east.

The Mexican forces moved forward, facing nothing but an open stretch of land and the black mouths of the cannons. The cannon shot tore through them. Dozens of men were wounded or killed within moments. Others pulled back, straight into the bayonets of their fellow attackers.

The cannons forced the Mexicans to the north side of the fort, right into the fire of their own attacking troops. Three battalions met in a mass under the north wall. Before long, the soldiers could no longer distinguish the voices of their commanders — and they mistakenly struck out at the men beside them.

To the south, the Mexican troops could not get close to the wall. It was protected by a trench and a wall of tangled brush that would slow them down and make them easy targets. The soldiers split up and edged west. They stayed well away from the palisade, where sharpshooting Crockett and his soldiers were firing with the fury of a hundred men.

The flash and crackle of rifles and the boom of cannon fire were like deafening thunder. The noise echoed off the walls, and the air filled with smoke and the muddled shouts and curses of men screaming in Spanish and English. Above it all rang the high-pitched screams of the horses and cattle in the corral. The ground trembled and the animals stamped in terror.

Below the north wall, Santa Anna's troops kept coming with their crowbars, picks, and ladders. For every man that fell, it seemed that two more appeared. They tore their hands on the rough timbers of their ladders. They climbed on one another's shoulders or clambered over the broken and bleeding bodies of the dead lying at the foot of the wall. Each time they reached the top of the wall, they faced the plunge of a bayonet, the club of a rifle butt, or the blow of a hatchet, as the Texians lashed out at their attackers.

❧

Smoke, noise, and cannon fire fill the air as the defenders battle the waves of Mexican soldiers pouring over the Alamo's walls.

CHAPTER THREE

OVER THE WALL

ROM THE NORTHERN BATTERY, SANTA ANNA SURVEYED THE BATTLE. SMOKE HUNG OVER the fort like an eerie mist, lit up by gunfire and by the dawn that was just beginning to break. He could see that three of his columns had collided. His men were stalled at the foot of the north wall, being picked off by the defenders on the roof. Enough was enough. It was time to send in his reserve forces to finish the job.

COLONEL TRAVIS AND JOE FIRED AT THE MEXICAN SOLDIERS FROM THE TOP OF THE NORTH WALL. They had kept the Mexicans at bay, but in all the dust and smoke it was getting harder and harder to see. Travis was behind the cannon, firing at the enemy and cheering on his men at the same time.

And then suddenly Colonel Travis was on the ground, slumped over. He had been shot in the head.

Things began to happen too quickly. There were more ladders against the wall, and in the next instant the Mexicans were scrambling over the top. The Texians on the roof of the barracks turned to shoot at them from inside, but there were too many. As Joe watched in horror, a Mexican officer loomed over Travis and slashed the colonel with his sword.

With Colonel Travis dead, Joe ran back across the courtyard and found shelter in one of the rooms in the west wall.

The Mexicans were coming over the walls on all sides, swarming into the fort. Some headed toward Crockett and his men at the palisade, now firing at the enemy on the inside.

With their bayonets poised, Santa Anna's forces charge fiercely across the open courtyard,
quickly overwhelming the outnumbered Texians.

They opened the main gate, and more soldiers poured in. They found Bowie lying on his sickbed. Too weak to hold a rifle, he had a pistol in each hand. He raised himself up and fired at the doorway, killing two Mexicans before more rushed in and stabbed him with their bayonets.

The Mexican soldiers were finally inside the Alamo. For this they had suffered the long march across the treacherous rivers, the hunger and cold, and the temper of their leader. Santa Anna had said there would be no mercy, and so there would be none.

The attackers thrust their bayonets in every direction. Faces and clothing were so blackened with powder and blood and smoke that no one could tell friend from foe. In the confusion they mistakenly turned on one another, firing on their own comrades and officers. Some were trampled to death. They ripped clothing, money, watches, and jewelry from the dead and wounded.

The Texians fought furiously, swinging their rifles and muskets, slashing with their knives. But they were hugely outnumbered. They sought cover in the barracks and were forced from room to room, until there was no place left to run.

At last only the church was left. The Mexicans swung one of the Alamo's own cannons toward the sandbags and dirt and wood that had been piled in front of the door. Then they blasted their way in.

Enrique and the others were in the sacristy. It was pitch-black in the room, and all he could hear were the screams and shouts outside. The Texians were shooting at the Mexicans as they came into the church. Then they swung their empty rifles like clubs when their attackers were right upon them.

Enrique could hear the shouts and thundering footsteps of the Mexican soldiers lining up at the foot of the ramp. He heard

Santa Anna's men storm the Alamo from every direction.

them fire. They were shooting at his father at the top of the ramp. He heard cries and the thud of bodies falling.

Enrique crawled under a pile of hay and closed his eyes. He put his hands over his ears. But he couldn't block out the awful sights and sounds.

Then the soldiers came through the door like a swarm of bees. They fired blindly into the room, their eyes unaccustomed to the dark.

Benjamin Wolfe was wrapped in a blanket, huddled in a corner nearby. When he heard the shots, he suddenly scrambled to his feet. Before Enrique could take a breath, he saw the fire from the barrel of a Mexican musket. He heard Benjamin's cry of surprise and pain as he fell heavily against Enrique.

Susanna Dickinson was huddled on her cot beside the door, bent over her baby. Suddenly a young artilleryman, Jacob Walker, staggered through the door, bleeding. He stumbled and fell against her. Susanna raised her head then, just in time to see the Mexican soldiers shoot Jacob again and toss him into the air with their bayonets as if he were a bundle of hay on a pitchfork.

WHEN THE FIRING HAD STOPPED, SANTA ANNA ENTERED THE ALAMO. ONE OF HIS GENERALS brought forward a group of Texian prisoners who had laid down their weapons and surrendered.

The president was furious. "What right have you to disobey my orders? I want no prisoners!" he shouted. He ordered them to be killed, then turned his back and walked away.

As Santa Anna's men attacked the defenders with their bayonets and knives, Colonel Almonte and several of the other officers turned away with tears in their eyes.

But Santa Anna had no mercy for the rebels. Travis had chosen to stand or die. Now the Texians were paying for that decision.

Only a few were spared, including Joe, who had been hiding in one of the rooms during the bloody scene. He was taken to Santa Anna's headquarters in town and questioned on all that he knew about Texas and its army. Brigado Guerrero, a Tejano man, convinced the Mexican soldiers that he was a Mexican prisoner of the Texians. He was also released.

Sitting proudly in his saddle, Santa Anna orders the execution of the few surviving rebels who have just surrendered.

CHAPTER FOUR

THE DEAD

B Y THE TIME THE SUN WAS FULLY UP ON MARCH 6, THE FIGHTING WAS OVER. BUT THE sights, sounds, and smells that remained were almost worse than the battle itself. There were moans of pain from the wounded, cries of grief, smoke, blood, and the smell of death. Scattered weapons and bullets lay everywhere, as well as broken bodies, some still burning.

So many were dead — defenders and attackers both.

Santa Anna walked through the fort, stepping over the corpses. It was a terrible sight to behold, even for him. He climbed to the top of one of the cannon posts while his troops lined up in formation around him.

He commended his men for their bravery. They had met with stubborn resistance from the enemy, but they had fought heroically and would be rewarded with the gratitude of the Mexican nation. It was true they had suffered many casualties, but this was the price of war. After all, the enemy had been protected by the walls of a fort, while his men had nothing but their own breasts to shield them. Besides, not a single Texian in the Alamo was left alive. They had achieved a complete and glorious triumph after less than two hours of fighting.

To the ragged and exhausted soldiers, it didn't feel much like victory. As Colonel Almonte accompanied the president and counted the dead, he knew that another such victory would ruin them. As many as five hundred Mexican soldiers were dead or wounded. The moans of their injured comrades came from every corner. The experienced soldiers among them knew that without enough medicine, doctors, beds, or blankets, those men were worse off than the dead.

But Santa Anna did not seem to notice the halfhearted cheers of his men. He ordered them to get rid of the bodies. Then he mounted his horse and headed across the river to his headquarters.

INSIDE THE CHURCH, ENRIQUE ESPARZA HUDDLED IN A CORNER WITH THE OTHERS AND TRIED NOT to look at the dead bodies in the room. The Mexican soldiers had left and the firing had stopped, but no one had come for them.

So they waited, stiff with terror, until the soldiers returned. The women and children were led outside.

Beside the ramp lay the crumpled body of Gregorio Esparza. Enrique's mother cried out and ran over. Enrique and his brothers and sister clung to her skirts until one of Santa Anna's men pulled them away.

The walls of the Alamo were splattered with blood. The doors and the palisade were splintered and battered. The air was still filled with the bitter smell of powder and smoke. As they passed Bowie's sickroom near the main gate, Enrique could see Bowie's body lying on the floor beside his cot, covered with blood.

Suddenly Enrique was gripped by a quiet, cold fear. "We must hold the Alamo," he remembered Bowie saying. "We must keep Santa Anna back. If we don't, even the women and children will be murdered."

Enrique and the others were taken to town. In the afternoon, they were summoned to appear before Santa Anna one family at a time. On the table in front of the president were a pile of blankets and stacks of silver coins.

Enrique looked across the table into the face of the same man he had seen riding into the main plaza two weeks before. At the Alamo, the Texians had told the boy that Santa Anna would cut off his ears if he ever caught him.

Enrique's mother was very sad and very quiet, but she was not afraid of Santa Anna.

"Why do you fight your countrymen?" Santa Anna asked her.

"They are not our countrymen," Ana Esparza said. "We are Tejanos."

"I suppose if I let you go, you will raise your children to fight Mexico."

"Yes," his mother answered.

"Get the mob out!" Santa Anna said, and he gave them a blanket and two silver coins and let the family go.

SUSANNA DICKINSON KNEW HER HUSBAND WAS DEAD. SHE WAS ALMOST AFRAID TO LEAVE THE dank, dark room that had been her home for two weeks. No one wanted to admit they were Americans.

Then one of the Mexican officers, Colonel Almonte, called to her in English.

"If you wish to save your life," he said, "follow me."

Clutching Angelina to her, she walked out into the daylight and saw the countless dead lying on the ground in front of the church. Some still clutched their swords and pistols. Some were so covered with blood and dirt that she could not tell which side they had been on.

Susanna buried Angelina's face in her shawl. Blood pooled on the sunbaked ground. She recognized the body of Crockett, his coonskin cap lying by his side.

Colonel Almonte led her out of the fort and gave her a horse that would take her back into town. "We are fighting men, not women," he said.

When Susanna was summoned to Santa Anna's headquarters, her skirts were still crusty with Jacob Walker's blood. She shrank back when Santa Anna reached out to pat Angelina. Then he said he would take Susanna and the baby back to Mexico City with him, where he would raise Angelina as his own daughter. She would be given a good education and fine clothes. The two of them would never want for anything for the rest of their lives.

Susanna was outraged. How could he presume such a thing, this man who was responsible for the death of her husband?

Once again, Colonel Almonte stepped in. He pointed out that he himself had been treated with great kindness when he was educated by the Americans in New Orleans. Would this not be a time for Santa Anna to show kindness as well, by letting Susanna go?

The Mexican president considered. Finally he nodded. Señora Dickinson would be given a horse and escorted out of town with Ben, one of Santa Anna's servants, to meet up with the Texians who were on their way to help with the fight.

He would send an Alamo widow to take the news of the defeat to the Americans.

Susanna Dickinson, who saw people she knew and loved lying dead inside the fortress, doesn't know what to expect from Santa Anna.

CHAPTER FIVE

Remember THE ALAMO!

A T THE SAME MOMENT THAT SANTA ANNA WAS CLAIMING VICTORY, GENERAL SAM HOUSTON, commander-in-chief of the Texian rebel army, was 176 miles away gathering his troops. He headed in the direction of San Antonio and rode late into the night. At dawn, he got off his horse and put his ear to the ground. Travis had vowed that as long as the Alamo could hold out, a cannon shot would be fired from the fort three times a day.

But Houston heard no cannons from the direction of the Alamo. He continued to gather his army and press on, but he was too late. He never made it to San Antonio. On March 11, he learned of the Alamo's defeat. The next day, he met up with Susanna Dickinson, Ben, and Joe, who had joined them on the road outside San Antonio.

Only women, children, slaves, and one Tejano man had been spared. Travis, Crockett, Bowie, and at least 186 of their fellow combatants were dead. Their bodies were gathered and burned. Funeral pyres were lit on either side of the cottonwood-lined road that led out of town. The fires blazed for days as the thick black clouds of evil-smelling smoke billowed up and spread over San Antonio.

Help from the rest of Texas and America did not arrive in time to save Travis and his men. But the two-week standoff at the Alamo allowed Texians a victory of another sort. While Travis held off the Mexican army, politicians gathered to draft the Texas Declaration of Independence and form a revolutionary government. News of the fall of the Alamo spread across the country to the east coast. Americans were outraged at the death of men like Crockett, Travis, and Bowie. They also mourned the loss of their own hometown sons, since the Alamo defenders had come from almost every state in the union. American anger against Santa Anna grew, as did the calls for revenge.

After the battle of the Alamo, the Mexican army pressed on into Texas. Six weeks later, Sam Houston's Texian army captured Santa Anna at San Jacinto. The battle was won after only twenty minutes. But for a long time after that, the Texians continued to chase down the Mexicans with guns, hunting knives, and bayonets. "Remember the Alamo!" they cried, as they killed 630 Mexican soldiers and captured 730 more.

The feuding over Texas continued for several years. Finally, in 1845, Texas became the twenty-eighth state. But Mexico refused to accept Texas independence, and the following year Mexico and the United States officially went to war.

By the time the Mexican-American War was over in 1848, Mexico had lost more than half of its once vast territory — including Texas, New Mexico, California, Utah, Nevada, Arizona, and parts of Colorado and Wyoming — and the United States had extended its domain all the way to the Pacific Ocean.

America and Mexico: 1848

The red section shows the area that the United States won from Mexico after the Mexican-American War. It wasn't long before several new states were established.

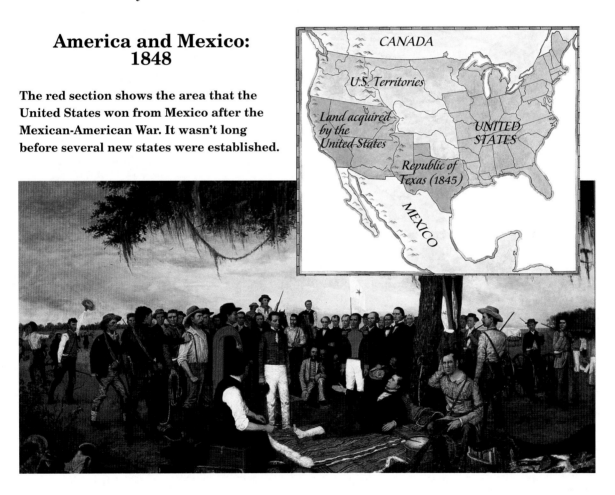

Santa Anna, captured at the battle of San Jacinto, is brought before Sam Houston, who has been injured in the fighting. The Mexican leader promises to remove all his troops from Texas if he is freed.

The Alamo: A Rebel Fortress

The Alamo was built in 1724 as a Catholic mission. The church and buildings housed the missionaries who came to New Spain to bring Christianity to the Native peoples. The walls of the mission were built as a defense against Comanche raids.

In 1793, the mission was closed, and the Alamo became a military garrison. The fort was an important outpost on the Mexican frontier until the Texians seized it in December 1835. This illustration shows how the Texians utilized the old mission during the siege and battle of the Alamo.

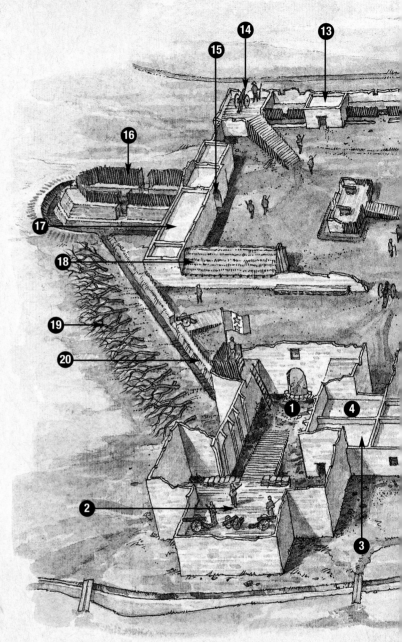

1. The Alamo church. The roof was never completed by the Spanish missionaries who built the Alamo.

2. A gun platform and ramp. The high mound and the ramp were built by the Mexican army before the Texians took over the Alamo.

3. The sacristy. During the siege, many of the women and children stayed here, including Susanna Dickinson and Enrique Esparza.

4. A storeroom for bushels of corn.

5. The horse corral.

6. The latrines.

7. The cattle pen. About thirty cattle were brought inside the Alamo when the siege began.

8. The long barracks where the infantrymen and artillerymen stayed.

9. The gun platform where William Travis and Joe fought.

10. Holes through which the cannons were fired.

11. The officers' quarters.

12. The fortress headquarters, where Colonel Travis stayed.

13. The artillery command post. Cannons were repaired here. This room also stored iron tools and wood.

14. The southwest corner where the largest cannon sat on a high platform.

15. The main gate into the Alamo.

16. The lunette. This semicircular wall, made of earth piled up against wooden stakes, helped protect the main gate.

17. The low barracks where James Bowie stayed after he became too ill to command the Alamo.

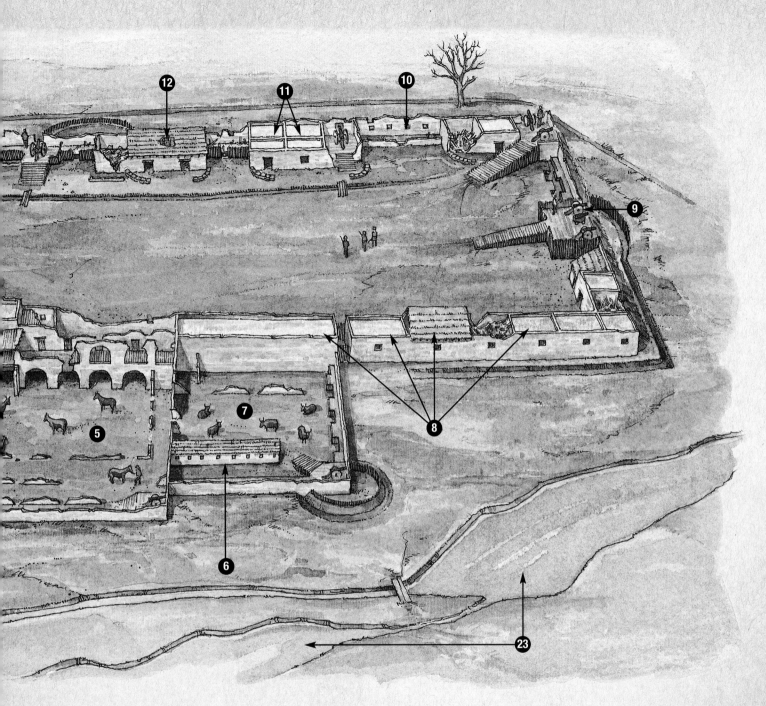

18. The kitchens.

19. A wall of trees, laid side by side and with sharpened branches, was built to keep the attackers back.

20. The south palisade. A fence of sharpened stakes, about eight feet high, where David Crockett and his men fought.

21. A well dug during the siege to provide water to those trapped in the Alamo.

22. The second floor of this building was used as a hospital; the first floor stored weapons.

23. These large ditches became an important source of water during the siege when the well inside the Alamo ran dry.

THE ALAMO
Remembered

TODAY NOT MUCH REMAINS OF THE sprawling Alamo fortress. But the church is still there. It sits surrounded by hotels, shops, and office buildings in the middle of San Antonio — a city where six out of ten people are now Tejanos of Mexican ancestry.

At the entrance to the church, visitors are asked to remove their hats as a sign of respect. It is cool inside the thick limestone walls. The church has been carefully restored. A roof now arches over the big room where cannons were once pushed up a dirt ramp to the battlements above.

Inside the church in the sacristy is a display case that contains a gold ring. It is the same cat's-eye ring that Colonel Travis gave to baby Angelina Dickinson just before the battle.

The ring (left) that Travis tied around Angelina's neck can be seen today at the Alamo (right).

40

Legends of the Alamo

The survivors of the Alamo told the world what had happened behind the walls during the battle. But because of the confusion and horror of the day, as well as tricks of memory, even the eyewitnesses did not agree. Some survivors told their stories to reporters, who made the accounts more thrilling so they could sell more newspapers. Some tales were repeated so often that soon the eyewitnesses themselves believed them, though they couldn't really remember.

Perhaps the most famous Alamo legend describes Colonel Travis talking to his men the night before the attack. Travis took out his sword and drew a line in the sand. Those who wanted to stay and fight could step across this line, he said. It would likely be a fight to the death. Only two men did not step up to cross the line. One was Louis Rose, who climbed the wall and disappeared. The other was James Bowie, who was too sick to walk. According to legend, he asked his fellow soldiers to carry his bed across the line, and they did.

One of the most colorful "eyewitness" accounts came from Madam Candelaria, a Mexican woman who

Travis watches as his men march across the famous line in the sand — a scene that likely never happened.

A dozen or so Mexicans sprang into the room occupied by Colonel Bowie. He emptied his pistols in their faces and killed two of them. As they lunged toward him with their muskets, I threw myself in front of them and received two of their bayonets in my body. One passed through my arm and the other through the flesh of my chin.... I implored them not to murder a sick man, but they thrust me out of the way and butchered my friend before my eyes....
I walked out of the cell and when I stepped upon the floor of the Alamo, the blood ran into my shoes.

— Madam Candelaria

claimed that she had been in the Alamo during the siege and nursed the sick James Bowie. In one interview, she described Mexican soldiers thrusting a bayonet into Bowie's body and lifting him right off the bed. In another, she showed off scars from injuries she claimed she had suffered when the Mexicans stormed Bowie's room.

Today, few historians believe that Madam Candelaria was even at the Alamo when it fell. And most doubt that the line-in-the-sand story is true.

As for David Crockett, many different stories were told about his death. Some said he died heroically while defending the palisade. Others claimed he was captured and executed after the battle on Santa Anna's orders.

This 1903 painting depicts David Crockett swinging his rifle butt over his head as he goes down fighting. But how Crockett actually died is still unknown.

The Rest of their Story

Enrique Esparza became a farmer when he grew up. He married and raised seven children and later moved back to San Antonio to live. When he was seventy-four years old, he told his story for the first time to a San Antonio newspaper. The year was 1902, and more than sixty-five years had passed since the famous siege and battle.

Enrique Esparza

After the battle of the Alamo, Susanna Dickinson moved eastward with several other Texian families fleeing the advancing Mexican army. Alone and penniless, she later made her way to Houston, where she applied for a widow's pension from the Texas government, but was denied. Susanna remarried four times and lived the last years of her life in Austin, Texas. She died in 1883 at the age of sixty-seven.

Susanna Dickinson

Angelina Dickinson was known as the Babe of the Alamo. She married at the age of seventeen and had three children before the marriage ended in divorce. She left her children with her mother and her uncle and went to live a wild and uncertain life in New Orleans. In her twenties, she fell in love and gave her sweetheart the cat's-eye ring that Colonel Travis had given her at the Alamo. The ring changed hands several times before it came to the Alamo, where it can be seen today.

Angelina Dickinson

The Alamo through the Years

1849 — (Left) This is the earliest known photograph of the Alamo, taken in 1849. Soon afterward, the bell-shaped facade on the front of the church was added to disguise the slope of the roof.

1866 — (Right, top) From 1849 to 1876, the U.S. Army used the Alamo as a supply base.

1888 — (Right, bottom) In the late 1800s, the Alamo's barracks were converted into a general store. In 1905, the Alamo was restored to its original stone structure and became a memorial to the people who fought at the Alamo. It is looked after by the Daughters of the Republic of Texas.

1935 — (Below) In the 1920s and '30s, several properties around the Alamo were bought and a memorial park was created. In 1936, President Franklin D. Roosevelt and his wife, Eleanor, visited the site during centennial celebrations.

GLOSSARY

adobe: a type of brick made of clay, earth, and straw.

ammunition: materials, such as bullets, that are fired from weapons.

artillerymen: soldiers who fight with weapons.

bayonet: a sharp steel blade attached to the end of a rifle.

cartridge: a container holding an explosive charge for a weapon.

colonist: a person who settles in a new country.

flint: a hard rock used for making a spark to ignite a gun.

garrison: a military post.

howitzer: a type of cannon.

mesquite: a type of small spiny tree or shrub found in areas from South America into the southwestern United States.

musket: a large gun that is carried on a soldier's shoulder and loaded with gunpowder through its muzzle.

palisade: a fence made of stakes sharpened at the top.

reinforcements: soldiers sent to strengthen an army.

republic: a nation in which the public elects a president to carry out laws.

sacristy: a room in a church in which sacred articles are kept.

siege: a blockade surrounding a fortress or city in an effort to make it surrender.

soldado: a Mexican soldier.

Tejano: a Mexican-born person living in Texas.

Texian: an American- or European-born person living in Texas.

INDEX

PICTURE CREDITS

All paintings are by David Craig unless otherwise indicated. All maps are by Jack McMaster.

C/M — CORBIS/MAGMA

CAH — Center for American History, University of Texas at Austin

DRT — The Daughters of the Republic of Texas Library

TSL — Texas State Library and Archives Commission

Front flap: DRT
1: North Wind Picture Archive.
8: Bettmann/C/M.
9: TSL.
13: Joseph Musso Collection.
15: TSL.
16: North Wind Picture Archives.
17: (Left and inset) DRT. (Right) TSL.
37: (Bottom) TSL.
40: The Alamo.
40–41: Gerald French/C/M.
42: DRT.
43: "Fall of the Alamo," 1903, by Robert Jenkins Onderdonk. Courtesy of Friends of the Governor's Mansion, Austin.
44: (Left and bottom right) DRT. (Top right) CAH.
45: (Top) CAH. (Second from top) The University of Texas Institute of Texan Cultures at San Antonio. No. 1228-E. The San Antonio Light Collection. (Third from top) DRT. (Bottom) Harry Ransom Humanities Research Center. The University of Texas at Austin.

RECOMMENDED READING

For young readers:

The Alamo: A Primary Source History of the Legendary Texas Mission by Janey Levy (Rosen Publishing Group). Recalls the experiences of those who fought at the Alamo.

Alamo (Sieges that Changed the World series) by Tim McNeese (Chelsea House). An exciting and informative account of the siege.

Inside the Alamo by Jim Murphy (Delacorte Press). A vivid history of the famous battle.

The Siege of the Alamo (Landmark Events in American History series) by Valerie J. Weber and Janet Riehecky (Gareth Stevens). The story of the Americans and Texians who fought the Mexican government for control of Texas.

For older readers:

The Blood of Noble Men: The Alamo Siege and Battle by Alan C. Huffines (Eakin Publications). An engrossing illustrated chronology of the thirteen-day siege.

WEBSITES

The Alamo *(official site)*
www.thealamo.org

Daughters of the Republic of Texas Library
www.drtl.org

ACKNOWLEDGMENTS

The text of this book, including any dialogue, is based on first-person accounts found in several sources, including *Eyewitness to the Alamo* by Bill Groneman, *The Blood of Noble Men: The Alamo Siege and Battle* by Alan C. Huffines, *The Alamo Remembered: Tejano Accounts and Perspectives* by Timothy M. Matovina, and *The Women and Children of the Alamo* by Crystal Sasse Ragsdale.

The author and Madison Press Books would like to thank John Anderson at the Texas State Library; Martha Utterback of the Daughters of the Republic of Texas; and Steven Williams at the Center for American History, University of Texas at Austin.

Editorial Director:
Hugh M. Brewster

Associate Editorial Director:
Wanda Nowakowska

Project Editor:
Kate Calder

Editorial Assistance:
Imoinda Romain

Graphic Designer:
Jennifer Lum

Production Director:
Susan Barrable

Production Manager:
Donna Chong

Color Separation:
Colour Technologies

Printing and Binding:
Tien Wah Press

THE ALAMO was produced by Madison Press Books, which is under the direction of Albert E. Cummings.

Madison Press Books
1000 Yonge Street, Suite 200, Toronto, Ontario, Canada, M4W 2K2